HOW TO BE LED BY THE HOLY SPIRIT

BY

PAUL NAUGHTON

Grosvenor House
Publishing Limited

The right of Paul Naughton to be identified as the author of this
work has been asserted in accordance with Section 78
of the Copyright, Designs and Patents Act 1988

The book cover is copyright to Paul Naughton

This book is published by
Grosvenor House Publishing Ltd
Link House
140 The Broadway, Tolworth, Surrey, KT6 7HT.
www.grosvenorhousepublishing.co.uk

A CIP record for this book
is available from the British Library

Paperback ISBN 978-1-83615-537-9
eBook ISBN 978-1-83615-538-6

This book is dedicated to my wonderful wife and my dear family, whose unconditional love has continually spurred me on to greater works.

THANK YOU

To my mentors who helped me become the Christian I am; to you, the reader, whose life I hope I will touch through this book; to my Lord and saviour, Jesus Christ, to whom I owe everything.

CONTENTS

The Road That Leads to Life   1

Born into the Supernatural   8

Your Unique Journey   20

The Word Lights the Way   26

God's Prayers for You   35

Baptised Into his Voice   48

Following his Leading   52

Attributes That Attract God   57

The 'F' Word   61

Set Apart for the Master's Use   69

His Presence   81

My Prayer for You

Heavenly Father,

As you have led me by Your Holy Spirit these many decades, I pray that you use the words in this book to raise up an army of determined, Spirit-led people, ready and willing to hear and obey Your voice; keep them from the hand of the enemy and from the voice of the deceiver; raise them up in purity of heart so they may see You and follow You; make them channels of Your peace and use them for Your glory. I ask this in the holy and glorious name of Jesus Christ, Your Son.

Amen.

Chapter 1

THE ROAD THAT LEADS TO LIFE

Sitting alone on my bed, my hands rested in my lap, as though I was going to receive something. A young man of 20, I waited in silence with my eyes closed, quietening my thoughts. *Psalm 62:1* was guiding me: "Truly my soul silently waits for God; from Him comes my salvation." With my eyes closed, I saw what looked like the light from a lantern in the distance coming towards me. As I called on the name of the Lord, the light got brighter and closer until I was completely enveloped in His glorious presence. An encounter like this marks you forever; I could never go back to life as usual.

The Treadmill

Many of us live far below our true potential. We wake up, get dressed, go to work, meet friends, come home, go to bed. Repeat. For some, they never escape the treadmill, going from birth to school, to work, to retirement, and, ultimately, to their death, without ever understanding (or fulfilling) their purpose. We live on a planet suspended in space, spinning relentlessly at 1,400 miles an hour, and go about our daily tasks, three meals a day, eight hours sleep a night, pursuing a fleeting feeling called 'happiness'. We save and spend, smile, laugh, cry, eat and drink, but often lack the joy of living every day in the knowledge of God's will.

Ecclesiastes 3:11 (AMP) reveals the Lord's desires for us all: "He has made everything beautiful in its time. He also has planted eternity in men's hearts and minds [a divinely implanted sense of a purpose working through the ages which nothing under the sun but God alone can satisfy]." When we live without a strong sense of mission, even our achievements can feel empty, and life's inevitable disappointments can bring us to a grinding halt. We often end up feeling that the abundant life for which Jesus died to provide, is just out of our reach. We ask ourselves: What's it all about?

If you have ever been arrested by God on your journey through life, you will realise that there's much more to life than all the drudge I mentioned above. But how do we enjoy God's very best? How do we live every day of our lives to the full? How do we fulfill our God-given destinies and ensure we eventually hear the words: "Well done, good and faithful servant!"? (*Matthew 25:23.*)

Levels of Relationship

There are varying degrees of relationship between God and His people. Some believers enjoy an intimacy that seems to evade others. There are those who live fruitful, rewarding lives, experiencing success in life and ministry, while many others struggle. Favour and blessings follow some while recurring issues cause others to stumble frequently. Others have an 'arm's length' relationship with their Heavenly Father.

All too often, people chase the wrong things at the wrong time and, as a result, their lives are out of sync with God's agenda. When you discover how to be led by the Holy Spirit, you will be able to enter a new season, and you will enjoy greater maturity in Christ.

I have written this book to help you grow in God and embrace your heavenly destiny. If you read this book with an open heart, I believe you will develop a deeper intimacy with the Lord and you will discover how to fulfill your highest purpose.

Thanks to the amazing favour of the Lord, it's possible to do God's will every day of your life. It's just as possible to live a godly, destiny-filled life today (more so) as it was in the days when we could have walked side by side with the Messiah. How do we know? Because the Bible says that where sin abounds around us, the favor of God abounds even more! (*Romans 5:20-21*).

Understanding God's favour towards us is a vital revelation in itself. We will approach this divine mystery later in the book.

The New You

The first step towards living life led by the Spirit of God is understanding your position in the "new creation' life. *2 Corinthians 5:17* says: "Therefore if anyone is in Christ, he is a new creature; the old things passed away; behold, new things have come." When we gave our lives to Christ, unless you received some kind of external miracle that changed your appearance, everything on the outside will have stayed very much the same.

There may be a new sparkle in your eye or a new spring in your step, but really, the changes will have happened in the realm of the unseen: the internal world, the spirit world. The change there is instantaneous and seismic. Like all big earthquakes, the effects can take a while to reach the surface of your life. The Holy Spirit is a gentleman; He requires your approval and your cooperation in your journey to newness of life.

Getting our heads around some of those seismic changes can be life-changing; the sheer extent of difference in the 'new' us can be overwhelming if we try to unbox them and walk them out all at once. So, like all good elephant-eating analogies, we'll digest them one bite at a time. The best place to start is to begin with who we now are. The Lord told me once that the biggest crisis in the body of Christ is an identity crisis. We don't know who we are! Many of us think and behave like we're just some old tramp who stumbled into a church, an old beggar who found bread, or a dying wretch who found 'grace'.

Your New Life

We may have started our new life in Christ that way, but when we said yes to Jesus, a series of laws as complex as the laws of gravity and elevation commenced their activities. Those lasting principles bring about change and transformation in every part of our lives. As we continue on this path called 'newness of life' by the Bible, these laws continue their remedial, transformational, and generational upgrade work.

The more we learn about these laws and embrace them (it's a bit like wearing the right clothing in the right season), the more we'll experience the glory of God in our daily lives.

So, who are we, then?

When you really grasp who you are, what you have been given, and what you are now capable of, it will change your life. *1 Peter 2:9* (*NKJV*) says: "But you are a chosen generation, a royal priesthood, a holy nation, His own special people, that you may proclaim the praises of Him who called you out of darkness into His marvellous light." These are not empty words – this is your new truth. The Bible says that you have been chosen; you have royal blood running through your veins, and you have been made holy. When you really understand who you are, it will become natural for you to walk in your supernatural purpose.

Limitless

The Bible says that you have been given limitless cognitive abilities: "… we have the mind of Christ." *(1 Corinthians 2:16.)* It doesn't stop there. *Deuteronomy 28:12b-13* says that the Lord will, "… bless all the work of your hand; and you shall lend to many nations, but you shall not borrow. The Lord will make you the head and not the tail, and you only will be above, and you will not be underneath, if you listen to the commandments of the Lord your God." In other words, your new life in Christ gives you access to unlimited mental resources; it gives you the opportunity to enjoy the favour of God upon the work of your hands, and offers you the opportunity to live in abundance, above your circumstances.

Knowing who you are and what God has given to you will help you adopt the right posture as you seek to be led by the Holy Spirit every day of your life. This book will help you to understand and fulfil your purpose; it will teach you how to follow the leading of the Lord as you navigate the twists and turns of life. It will show you how to live life His way, and how to embrace the multitude of blessings our Heavenly Father has provided. Following the leading of the Holy Spirit is the greatest and most exciting way to live!

Chapter 2

BORN INTO THE SUPERNATURAL

The Holy Spirit taught me how to follow His leading after an encounter with God that literally scared the hell out of me and changed the entire direction of my life. To help you understand my journey, I am going to share some of my testimony with you in this chapter. It will help you follow some of what I share later in this book.

I was born in London, England, during the baby boom of the mid 1960s. My father was a strict, devout Irish Catholic man while my mother was an English rose. Sandwiched in between two sisters, I was the only boy. My family lived in a cold, damp council house with no inside toilet, running hot water or central heating. My constant bedwetting made for the strangest odour, especially when I only had a bath every few months. Our clothes were second-hand, jumble sale leftovers, scavenged or sometimes donated by neighbours who pitied us.

Religion only reinforced our wretched lifestyle. One of the Catholic vows is poverty. We were dutifully dragged to church every Sunday to participate in Mass. Woe betide if we ever acted up during Mass. Trouble sometimes meant a telling off, but at times my father used excessive violence towards us kids. It was often a shocking bolt out of the blue, creating almost constant tension. For no reason at all, cups would go flying and plates would become missiles. Silly mistakes (like jam on the outside of the jar) resulted in severe beatings with fists or sticks.

There is still a sizeable piece of bone missing from my leg where my dad threw a boulder at me for breaking something I hadn't broken; my lower jaw hangs looser than it should because he punched me in the face one night. I quickly connected his devotion to religion as the cause for his behaviour, so, to me, God was an angry masochist who bred haters and hypocrites. I rejected God. My mother, on the other hand, was an unconditionally loving diamond of a lady. Everything around her exuded love, acceptance and kindness. She became a protective barrier from the worst of my dad's character flaws and a shining example of how to love. Dysfunction and poverty were our hallmarks, but Mum was our pain relief.

We moved from our broken-down, uninhabitable wreck of a house in a leafy suburb of London to a newly built, four-bedroom townhouse with central heating and two toilets inside. But it was located in a hellhole neighbourhood called Tottenham. Things went crazy from there. Somebody high up in our local municipality probably had the idea that if they mixed all the troubled families with a few good ones, everyone would end up nice and righteous. Of course, the opposite happened. Criminality was rife.

A Cruel, Criminal Culture

Every day, something went on in our neighbourhood: domestic violence, stolen goods being sold door to door, wholesale drug dealing, prostitution, muggings, robberies, street fights, road rage, burglaries. The list went on. The Irish political scene had reached a febrile state as well. The hunger strikers were at their worst, and bombings, shootings and reprisals were in full swing. The IRA membership that my dad had relinquished in the late 1960s to focus on raising us, was starting to itch him again.

Life was anarchy and the meanest ones were top of the heap. Severe bullying at school finished off the hardening of my heart. In my teenage years, I transitioned from a sweet, playful child into a hard-hearted, streetwise, pitiless psycho. When my father died shortly after my 16th birthday in 1982, that generational curse of rebellion landed on me. I had a fight with the local priest because he wouldn't allow the Irish flag, black beret and gloves on my dad's coffin (the symbol of a fallen Irish Republican terrorist) to honour his work in the 'Borstal Boy' bombing campaign in London in the 1950s.

My inner sense of utter worthlessness was reinforced by prolonged periods of unemployment; there were no jobs for people raised in my neighbourhood with hardly any qualifications. Desperately seeking significance, I decided I would do my part for Irish 'freedom', so I became heavily baptised into Irish politics. I started to swallow books on the armed struggle, chose my heroes, and decided that I'd become an armed robber for 'the cause'. I started buying a weekly newspaper where bombs were described as 'devices', terrorists were called 'volunteers' and dead prisoners were 'martyrs'.

Divine Appointment

My cousins in Ireland were crazier than I was. Although not politically engaged, life with them was always colourful. With 10 children living in a three-bedroom house, the atmosphere was wildly chaotic. Their father, my dad's brother, was an alcoholic who would slow boil, and then, in a fit of rage, launch whatever was nearby towards his intended target. Fights regularly erupted between siblings and their poverty was worse than ours.

One of the boys in the family was called Mike. Mike stayed with us in London one summer, and even though my dad hated his guts, one evening, he turned to my cousin and told him that it was important to pray to the Holy Spirit. My cousin was freaked out but did what he was told. That night he whispered, "Holy Spirit, I don't exactly know what I'm doing, but Uncle Cecil said I should pray to you, so here I am." He continued for a while then went to sleep. The next day, a friend of ours from down the road in Tottenham knocked at our door looking for Mike. "I've just finished this book and I think you'd like it," she said, and handed him a copy of *Run Baby Run* by Nicky Cruz.

Cruz was a hardened drug dealer in urban New York City whose life was radically transformed by a pastor from Times Square Church called David Wilkerson. Mike devoured the book. When he reached the part where the author led readers to say the Sinner's Prayer, Mike invited Jesus into his heart, then rolled over to go to sleep. The next morning, everything had changed: years of burden, confusion, tension, and hate seemed to have just melted away. A sea of peace washed over Mike, and a new serenity entered his life. Upon his return to Ireland at the end of that summer, he found a handful of 'believers' and attended the Christian meetings he could find.

Summer of Salvation

The summer of '84, I arrived at my cousins' front door for my annual vacation. When my cousin Tina opened the door, I knew instantly that something had changed. There was a quietness and a stillness, a serenity and peace, like you feel when you visit a family with a newborn baby. My mind started racing. *There's no way any of the girls has had a baby outside of marriage, my uncle would have killed them,* I thought. Eventually, I asked straight out, "So, what's gone on here, then?"

With a big beaming smile, she answered, 'We've met Jesus, Paul!'

My face felt like it dropped a 1000 metres in an instant. I made my excuses, went to the room to put my suitcase away, and set about my strategy to wake them up out of whatever nonsense they were into now. I decided I would work on my closest cousin, Nick, as we were like brothers, so I took him for a spin in my car around Galway Town. He spent the whole journey telling me what had happened: Mike had persuaded three of the girls to come on vacation with him to a charismatic renewal camp. Their vacation was life-changing.

As the camp trip went on, a guy from Dublin in a neighbouring caravan, called Paul Kelly, invited three of my cousins to his prayer meeting. The Holy Spirit came down during that prayer meeting – suddenly and powerfully! Instantly, they were swept into the presence of God, baptised in the Holy Spirit, and began speaking in tongues, having visions, repenting of their sins. The whole lot! When they came back from this experience and told their family, they could hardly talk. The entire household was swept into the presence of God, and it stayed there. All 10 children in the family were now in some level or other of encounter with God.

And there I was, with my plans for a wild two weeks of debauchery, loaded with cash I had saved up, ready to tear up the town once again. I was deflated. My cousins used every available minute to update me on their latest revelation, telling me that God was going to visit me, and that when He does, I must say the Sinner's prayer. I laughed off their advances and instead decided to concentrate on some of their good-looking neighbours.

The Day my Life Changed

The two weeks passed by quickly, and the night before I was due to drive back to England, I dropped my latest girlfriend home and decided I would politely sit with my cousins for the last bit of the evening. I came into their house, made a cup of tea, and sat on the edge of their couch with my back to the door, which was slightly open.

I suddenly felt the presence of someone behind me. It felt like all the love I had ever experienced in my whole life was standing behind me in human form. I went as cold as stone. My mind started whirring. Had I drunk too much? Had someone spiked my drink? No. This is real. I froze. 'Lord, I'm sorry,' I said in my heart, 'I didn't know You were real!'

The words of my cousins came racing into my mind: *You're going to encounter Jesus, Paul, and, when you do, you have to say the Sinner's prayer.*

'Lord Jesus, I'm sorry for my sins. Come into my heart and make me a brand-new person.' As I said these words, it was as if somebody took a bottle of warm oil and poured it over my head. From being as cold as a gravestone, I felt like I had been wrapped in a warm blanket of love. My mind was *totally* freaked out!

As far as I could tell, my cousins were completely oblivious of everything that had just happened, but about five seconds after my experience, one of them said, 'Wow, I feel like the presence of Jesus has just walked into the room. Let's pray for Paul, as he goes back to London tomorrow.' This freaked me out even more, but my heart was enjoying wave after wave of love. They could feel this presence too and they were calling him Jesus! A couple of them said a nice 'safe journey' prayer and then I spoke up:

'Guys, I believe that God wants us to build His kingdom on Earth.' As I said those words, I wondered who had said them! It felt like that cartoonish situation whereby a guy says something then tries to wind back the words with a fishing reel. The whole thing felt crazy.

'That's Jesus speaking through you, Paul!' shouted Mike, rising from his seat and pointing his finger at me. My internal freakometre was now off the scale, but this love sensation, this sense of connection with Heaven, this peace that was now deep inside me, caused me to totally ignore my mind and enjoy this awesome serenity. As they continued their praying and chatting, I said my goodbyes, hugged them, and went to bed.

An Introduction to the Holy Spirit

Once back in London, I sold my car, gave up my real estate sales job, and jumped on a coach back to Ireland two weeks later. I knew if I stayed, I would be dragged back into my old debauched, criminal life. By the time I got back to Ireland, a move of God was sweeping through Galway. Upwards of 30 young people and a bunch of adults had come to Jesus in radical ways, and lives were being transformed.

We were in prayer meetings six days a week; we learned about the gifts of the Holy Spirit by operating in them, then realising that they were in the Bible! Books came flooding in and we started to realise that we weren't the only people on this planet who had this kind of experience with Jesus – there were millions of us! Those early days were tough, naturally speaking. Surviving on £35 a week, working for a man who used to introduce me as his 'slave', was gruelling. The cold, wind and rain in Galway would go straight through you and riding a bike three miles to and from work to my slave position was trying. But Jesus was beating strong in my life. If this was the life He had for me, then I was over the moon about it.

The Voice of God

The first time I heard the voice of God was in a post office in Galway Town while waiting in line. It was December 1984, three months after being gloriously baptised in The Holy Spirit and speaking in other tongues. Waiting in line to post a parcel home for Christmas, a song came over the radio: "I'll be home for Christmas." Suddenly, a warm sensation filled me, and I knew that I would be home for Christmas. I didn't know how—I was as broke as a joke—but I just knew! About a week later, a cousin called by the house.

'Paul, we're going to see my husband's family in London, and we have space in the car. Would you like a lift home?'

I was radiant with joy. The idea of going home to a warm, dry home with plenty of food was like Heaven on Earth to me. But what was even more awesome was that I had heard it from God a few weeks before it happened. My trust levels rocketed. If the Holy Spirit could lead me and guide me in such a small, irrelevant thing, He could lead me into all truth and show me things to come! He put me in that postal office; He had me there at exactly the right time; He inspired the DJ to play that exact song at that exact time.

I searched the Scriptures to make sure that what I was believing He had done, and, lo and behold, my bible was peppered with instances of God leading

His people supernaturally. I was on track. "Those who are being led by the Spirit of God are the sons of God." (*Romans 8:14.*) 'I want to be a son of Yours,' I used to pray, 'not a babe nor an infant, not a child, but a son!' Sonship became my goal; it meant maturing. I wanted to ace every test I came across to show Him I was a trustworthy candidate for sonship.

Sensitivity to Atmospheres

I hadn't realised it while I was growing up, but my sensitivity to atmospheres wasn't something everyone possessed: it was a spiritual rather than a natural attribute. I increasingly desired to operate in the gifts of the Holy Spirit, and the more I desired it, the more I saw it happen. Paul Kelly, the man at the camp who had sparked this move of God's Spirit, became our mentor. 16 of us would cram into his blue station wagon and go on ministry trips. These were the best of times.

Paul operated in the gifts of the Holy Spirit; he was as bold as a lion and attacked sickness in others like a wild man. He had an unusual love for fasting and a sense of purpose that propelled him into some amazing achievements. 'Lord,' I remember praying, 'I know it's you doing these marvellous things in these meetings. Please open my eyes to see what You're going to do before it happens.'

I started to look around at the people in the circle with their eyes closed, joining hands and praying in the Spirit. Slowly, but surely, I began to 'see' into the spiritual realm. I would sometimes see a cloud over people, sometimes a light, and I knew they'd be prayed for next. I was seeing the future! Next, I started to ask the Lord to show me what He would say or do through Paul while he was ministering. I would receive ideas or impressions of what was about to happen: I would know what Scripture was going to be read, or what teaching would come.

I was becoming a man of God myself.

My salvation was supernatural. My first steps as a believer gave me an awareness of the presence of the Holy Spirit, and my life since has been a walk of faith, following His leading. I count it a major privilege to now share with you some of the principles that have shaped my life.

Chapter 3

YOUR UNIQUE JOURNEY

Everyone has a personal journey with God, a story of salvation and Christian living. If you look closely, you will find clues about your future scattered throughout your Christian walk. As you look back at some of these signs along the way, you will see glimpses of your God-given destiny. These pointers will show you what kind of man, or woman, of God you're going to become. If you will look for God's 'fingerprints' in your life, it will help you focus on the things that are important for you (though not necessarily for your friends or family)! *Ephesians 2:10* explains that you have unique things to do for the Lord: "For we are His workmanship, created in Christ Jesus for good works, which God prepared beforehand so that we would walk in them."

Knowing your specific purpose will help you to prepare. *2 Timothy 2:21* says: "Therefore, if anyone cleanses himself from these things, he will be a vessel for honor, sanctified, useful to the Master, prepared for every good work." As you zoom in on God's specific priorities for you, you will be shaped into a vessel that is fit for the Master's use.

The Lord showed me diversity of gifts recently while I was in my kitchen. I could see a variety of electrical gadgets, each with a different purpose: a mixer, an air fryer, the toaster, kettle, and so on. Each appliance uses differing amounts of the same power with markedly different results. In the same way, we are all connected to the Holy Spirit, the source of our power, but He has shaped each of us for a unique purpose. *1 Corinthians 12:18 (TPT)* describes this principle: "But God has carefully designed each member and placed it in the body to function as He desires." Why not look back over your life right now? Ask the Lord to reveal the experiences and people that moulded your life and character. These can provide clues about your unique design and God's purpose for your life.

Life Shapers

My family used to visit an Irish Catholic men's club when I was a child. The chairman, a man called Jack Daly, made a lasting impression on me. I watched as he made everyone feel welcome, building genuine relationships with the regulars. He frequently diffused tensions between feisty Irishmen before aggression turned into a fight. At that time, it was normal practice for police to wait outside Irish venues, ready to intervene when fights kicked off. The police were never outside our club, though, because Jack Daly was like a pastor to his people. I believe that my meet-and-greet approach to pastoring was formed as an eight-year-old watching Jack Daly.

Who helped shape *your* life? Who made a lasting impression upon *you*? Who influenced *your* outlook or behaviour? What mark did they leave? How might their presence in your life have helped to prepare you for your purpose? Moses was raised by a princess in a palace that equipped him to face Pharaoh years later. What about you?

Developing Desire

One of the biggest factors affecting your relationship with the Holy Spirit is your level of desire. *James 1:14-15* explains the power of desire. When you persistently hunger after something, it causes a birthing on the inside. Jesus said: "Whatsoever things you desire when you pray, believe you receive them and you shall have them." (*Mark 11:24.*) If you long to be led by the Holy Spirit and make this a prayer point, you will then start to see your journey of following the Lord unfold.

If your current levels of hunger are somewhat muted, don't worry! You can develop desire for the things of God on the inside. Just as the smell of freshly baked bread can stir up an appetite, or the whiff of newly brewed coffee can pull you into a café, you can awaken spiritual hunger. Reading this book is an excellent way to create desire for the Lord. Hang around with people who are sensitive to the Holy Spirit, spend time in worship, and dig into the word. Be intentional about stirring passion.

How Does the Holy Spirit Speak?

You are unique. Just as no one has the same fingerprint, no two people have an identical personality. Of course, it was God who designed you, so He knows the very best way to communicate with you. I know people who 'hear' God through advertising billboards, radio adverts, pop songs and movies. Other folk see the Lord in the wonder of nature; others hear Him through their daily interactions.

John 3:6 makes an important statement: "That which is born of the flesh is flesh, and that which is born of the Spirit is spirit." Just like the Heavenly Father, you are a spirit. You have a soul, and you live in a body, but your essence is a spirit. The Holy Spirit speaks with your spirit, not with your soul. Like tuning into an old-fashioned radio, you can tune your spirit to hear the Holy Spirit. Radios in the old days even had a 'fine tune' button. It would be so handy to have a spiritual equivalent!

Yes, but how will I know if it's really Him?

I'm glad you asked! In *John 10:27*, Jesus said: "My sheep know my voice, they listen to my voice, they follow my voice and the voice of another they simply will not follow." In the next chapter, I will unpack the four promises God gives us in this verse. For now, allow the foundational truth of this Scripture to sink into your soul. According to the Lord Jesus Himself, you *do* hear His voice. The question is therefore not can I hear His voice, but *how* do I hear His voice?

Think about two or three occasions when you know you heard from God. How did He speak to you? Where were you? What were you doing at the time? Understanding *how* you heard the voice of the Lord in the past will help you to position yourself to hear Him again. A mighty man of God (who is also a dear friend of mine) hears the Lord most acutely when he is near water, so he bought an apartment beside the ocean. My wife feels the closeness of the Holy Spirit when she is alone in the countryside. Indeed, *Psalm 23:2* says: "He makes me to lie down in green pastures; He leads me beside the still waters."

Get Ready

Prepare yourself. God loves you just the way you are, but He loves you too much to leave you the way you are. If you're going to do this thing, do it. Dig out Scriptures that relate to hearing God's voice and recite them over your life in the first person: "Heavenly Father, thank you that I hear Jesus's voice, I know His voice, I follow His voice, and the voice of another I simply will not follow." (*John 10:27.*)

You were created by your Heavenly Father; you are not here by the plans of man, but by God's will and intention. You have a mandate to fulfill. You are unique, so you bring something unique to the earth. Even if you're a spiritual son or daughter of a great man or woman of God, you are not a clone. You need to follow the leading of the Holy Spirit every day of your life to ensure that you fulfill your divine purpose.

Chapter 4

THE WORD LIGHTS THE WAY

The word of God is the blueprint for your life; it is the map that will lead you to your destiny. It is impossible to believe what the Bible says and remain the same. Scripture is God's reprogramming software for our souls. His word rearranges our priorities according to His and changes our lives so that we become more like Him. As you dig into the word, allow it to challenge (and change) your character and let it redefine what is important to you so that you become a vessel fit for the Master's use.

I want to go back to a foundational verse on our topic I mentioned in the last chapter. *John 10:27* says: "My sheep know my voice, they listen to my voice, they follow my voice and the voice of another they simply will not follow." In this one Scripture, Jesus makes four phenomenal promises concerning His voice.

Promise One: My Sheep Hear my Voice

The majority of believers regularly doubt their ability to hear God's voice. Yet the word of God states in black and white (or red and white) that if you belong to Jesus, you do hear His voice! Instead of thinking you need to learn a new spiritual skill, understand that you already can hear His voice. You probably just need to discern which voice is His and discover how to quieten distracting noise.

Can we mishear God's voice? Of course. In truth, I think we all mishear Him from time to time. So, how can we avoid this happening? The short answer is by maturing in God. Let's look at how we can grow and, in so doing, protect ourselves from too much mishearing.

Firstly, get to know the Bible so that His word becomes your truth. That makes it easier to work out what is not God because He never contradicts Himself. Secondly, through worship and prayer, keep your spirit alive and alert. Thirdly, with the help of the Holy Spirit, seek to live a sanctified life. One of Jesus's last prayers before his death was: "Sanctify them [purify, consecrate, separate them for yourself, make them holy] by the truth; your word is truth." (*John 17:17 AMP.*) Fourthly, ask the Holy Spirit to make you aware of any wrong motivations. It's sad how many times we want to grow in God to look good or get noticed. Ask The Holy Spirit to do a deep work in you.

It's also important to keep your spirit ticking over, just like a car with the engine on, stationary but ready to go, idling, ticking over. I do this personally by praying in the spirit. If you haven't yet been filled with the Holy Spirit with the evidence of speaking in other tongues, I encourage you to ask God to baptise you with His spirit. *Luke 11:13* says: "If you then, being evil, know how to give good gifts to your children, how much more will your Heavenly Father give the Holy Spirit to those who ask Him!" Not only does He give you a new heavenly language, but the baptism in the Spirit brings great joy, peace and intimacy with the Lord.

Promise Two: They Know my Voice

The more tuned into the voice of God you become, the better. It's a constant process of listening out and tuning in. *Psalm 123:2* says: "Behold, as the eyes of servants look to the hand of their master, as the eyes of a maid to the hand of her mistress, so our eyes look to the Lord our God." This verse captures the joy of continual readiness and eagerness to hear His voice. Learn to hear God in the small things so that you are more confident when it comes to important decisions.

Sometimes, the voice of the Lord is as silent as the moving of an eye. We must be attentive, and we need to stay close to Him. *Psalm 32:8 (KJV)* says: "I will instruct thee and teach thee in the way which thou shalt go: I will guide thee with mine eye."

Promise Three: My Sheep Follow My Voice

The Lord trains us in obedience. He may prompt you to be kind to someone who is harsh; He could ask you to love a difficult family member. Perhaps He will convince you to leave every toilet cubicle better than you found it! He will almost certainly ask you to forgive someone who hurt you badly. It is in these small steps of obedience that we learn to follow His voice. Obedience usually costs something, and one day it could cost you everything. God also wants to give us His word for other people. It may be a joy when the Spirit leads you to declare, "I'm healing a guy with a chest infection right now, it's flying away like a bird!" But what about when he asks you to confront a fellow brother in love about the error of his ways?

You see, God's ways are asymmetrical – they don't often line up from a human perspective. He may well ask you to do something that is very hard or doesn't make sense. But your obedience could pave the way for God to meet a need six months down the road that you don't even know about at the time of your obedience.

Here's an example from Scripture: Moses was leading the children of Israel through the wilderness, and they needed water. They found a river but there was a problem: the water was bitter. 10 years earlier, when Moses was still in Egypt negotiating with Pharaoh, a tree seed blew through the wilderness. The heavens opened and it rained just when that seed landed near the river. The seed took root, shoots broke through the soil, and a tree began to grow. 10 years later, it became the solution to a problem for God's chosen people. "See that tree over there, Moses? Cut it down and throw it into the river and the water will be made sweet." (*Exodus 15: 22-25.*) May you become the answer for the bitterness of your generation! It starts with following the leading of the Holy Spirit.

Sharing His Voice

Sometimes, hearing His voice for a person, or people, can be a lonely place. We aren't all called to be prophets, but some are. Jeremiah saw where Israel was headed 23 years before his vision became a reality. They were moving towards disaster but couldn't see it. Many of satan's tricks to deceive people are having the same effect today. If God showed you the problems with a nation or a people, would you be willing to stand up and be a voice? Obedience often requires death to self and the laying down of your reputation. Are you willing to lay down yours?

There is a Bible principle called 'The law of the watchman'. This affects those who receive messages from God for His people. The Lord explained this principle to his prophet in *Ezekiel 33: 2-6 (NLT)*:

Son of man, give your people this message: 'When I bring an army against a country, the people of that land choose one of their own to be a watchman. When the watchman sees the enemy coming, he sounds the alarm to warn the people. Then if those who hear the alarm refuse to take action, it is their own fault if they die. They heard the alarm but ignored it, so the responsibility is theirs. If they had listened to the warning, they could have saved their lives. But if the watchman sees the enemy coming and doesn't sound the alarm to warn the people, he is responsible for their captivity. They will die in their sins, but I will hold the watchman responsible for their deaths.

Ezekiel knew that if he gave the people a word of correction from the Lord and the people ignored it, God would hold the people responsible. However, if Ezekiel withheld the word of the Lord, God would hold Ezekiel responsible for the behaviour of the people. If you want God to speak through you, it is important that you understand this precept. Settle the gravity of this principle in your heart before you ask God to make you His mouthpiece, because the consequences of withholding a word of warning can be huge.

Promise Four: The Voice of Another, They Will Not Follow

The fourth and final promise from *John 10:10* is the guardrail for all the other promises. It is a promise to those who will "wholly follow the Lord" (*Joshua 14:8*). If you are truly attentive, if you rid yourself of every agenda, if you free yourself from selfish ambition and any desire for recognition or glory, God will lead you every step of the way. He will protect you from contrary voices and guide you into His highest plans for your life.

In *1 Kings 19*, Elijah had an encounter with God. Thunderous winds blew, an earthquake shook the rocks, and a fire burned, but the Lord was not in the loud or the dramatic. That day, He spoke with a still, small voice. Sometimes, the voice of God is internal, like an inner whisper. But we cannot put God's voice into a so-called box. He will speak, but His voice will sound in different ways. *Psalm 29* says:

> The voice of the Lord is upon the waters; the God of glory thunders, The Lord is over many waters. The voice of the Lord is powerful, the voice of the Lord is majestic. The voice of the Lord breaks the cedars; yes, the Lord breaks in pieces the cedars of Lebanon… The voice of the Lord hews out flames of fire. The voice of the Lord shakes the wilderness; the Lord shakes the wilderness of Kadesh. The voice of the Lord makes the deer to calve and strips the forests bare; and in His temple everything says, 'Glory!'

We cannot stereotype the Holy Spirit as a sweet, gentle dove (*Matthew 3:16*) because the next time He manifested Himself, He appeared as a rushing mighty wind and tongues of fire! In the same way, the Lord speaks in different ways at different times. But His promise to you is that He will keep you on His path.

Integrity Protection

The integrity of our hearts is of the utmost importance when dealing with the things of God. *Proverbs 10:9* says: "He who walks in integrity walks securely, but he who perverts his ways will be found out." Motive is paramount. If we keep our hearts right, even when we get it wrong, God will see us through. Practicing hearing His voice is so wonderful. Ask Him what Scriptures to read, who to bless with a gift or an act of kindness; ask Him who you should call with a word of encouragement. When you seek His will and follow His voice in your daily life, He will lead you in a deeper love walk. He will draw closer to you as you draw closer to Him. (*James 4:8.*)

God's Highest Way

Our Heavenly Father's number one way of moving through us in the lives of others is via the medium of love. *1 Corinthians 12:31* calls it, "... a still more excellent way." Many times, God will tell us to do something out of love. He could ask us to love someone we would rather punch on the nose! But that's God's way. Doing things through love does something on the inside: it forms our character. God is often more interested in the process of transforming us than He is in what we do for others.

There may be times when we think we are sacrificing for God, but He has an eye on the outcome down the road. The story of the rich young ruler is a case in point. In *Mark 10:21*, the Bible says that Jesus loved him. He then told that young man to give up everything. As we read further on in the same chapter, we discover in verse 29 that Jesus would have made him 100 times richer, but for this man, the step of faith was too much.

Chapter 5

GOD'S PRAYERS FOR YOU

One unexpected benefit of praying with a friend is that you get to know them better. When a person prays, they share the desires of their heart with the Lord, so you get to hear what's important to them. Now, imagine eavesdropping while Jesus was interceding for you. You would hear His longings for your life; you would find out what matters most to Him. Well, you can! Seven times in the *New Testament*, we read the words: "I pray." Although the books of the Bible were written by different men, like Paul, Peter and John, "all Scripture is God breathed." (*2 Timothy 3:16.*) The Bible is the word of God, so these prayers may have been penned by men, but they are from the heart of God. I call them the seven prayers of the Holy Spirit.

This book is all about learning to follow the leading of the Lord. When you understand what matters most to God, it becomes much easier to discern His voice. In this chapter, we will look at the seven prayers the Holy Spirit prays for you and me. As we study these prayers, you will discover more of who you are in Christ. I call this, 'Geolocation in God's word'.

Geolocation is the process that GPS uses to show you where you are and how to get to where you're going. We can geolocate ourselves in the word of God using the seven prayers of the Holy Spirit. By hearing the cry of God's heart for you, you will discover where He wants you to be. If you pray daily in agreement with His prayers, it will be like inputting your desired destination into your life's GPS. Your prayers, together with the Holy Spirit's, will then lead you there. First, we will look at the seven prayers and then we will consider common themes.

One of the greatest things that I could ever encourage you to do is to say these prayers. As you continue through this chapter, don't just read the verses that follow, ingest them and turn them into prayers. Speak them over your loved ones and over your own life. They are more than just prayers, they carry an impartation of God's manifold wisdom and blessing. Ask the Lord to make these divine petitions come alive in your heart.

The Holy Spirit's First Prayer for You

In *Ephesians 1:15-23*, we hear the Holy Spirit's first prayer for you and me:

> For this reason I too, having heard of the faith in the Lord Jesus which exists among you and

your love for all the saints, do not cease giving thanks for you, while making mention of you in my prayers; that the God of our Lord Jesus Christ, the Father of glory, may give to you a spirit of wisdom and of revelation in the knowledge of Him. I pray that the eyes of your heart may be enlightened, so that you will know what is the hope of His calling, what are the riches of the glory of His inheritance in the saints, and what is the surpassing greatness of His power toward us who believe. These are in accordance with the working of the strength of His might which He brought about in Christ, when He raised Him from the dead and seated Him at His right hand in the heavenly places, far above all rule and authority and power and dominion, and every name that is named, not only in this age but also in the one to come. And He put all things in subjection under His feet and gave Him as head over all things to the church, which is His body, the fullness of Him who fills all in all.

The Holy Spirit's Second Prayer for You

This prayer reveals God's desire for you receive His strength so that you can fulfil His purposes. We hear His longing for you and I to really understand His love. In *Ephesians 3:14-21*, the Holy Spirit prays:

For this reason I bow my knees before the Father, from whom every family in Heaven and on earth derives its name, that He would grant you, according to the riches of His glory, to be strengthened with power through His Spirit in the inner man, so that Christ may dwell in your hearts through faith; and that you, being rooted and grounded in love, may be able to comprehend with all the saints what is the breadth and length and height and depth, and to know the love of Christ which surpasses knowledge, that you may be filled up to all the fullness of God. Now to Him who is able to do far more abundantly beyond all that we ask or think, according to the power that works within us, to Him be the glory in the church and in Christ Jesus to all generations forever and ever. Amen.

The Holy Spirit's Third Prayer for You

Our God always has an eye on eternity and ensuring we are prepared and qualified. *Philippians 1:9-11* says:

And this I pray, that your love may abound still more and more in real knowledge and all discernment, so that you may approve the things that are excellent, in order to be sincere and blameless until the day of Christ; having been filled with the fruit of righteousness which comes through Jesus Christ, to the glory and praise of God.

The phrase translated "approve the things that are excellent" literally means to be able to distinguish between the things that differ. The Lord desires that you can discern even subtle differences so that you can make Holy Spirit-led choices.

The Holy Spirit's Fourth Prayer for You

You fulfilling your calling is very much on the heart of God. Listen to His longing in *Colossians 1:9-14*:

> For this reason also, since the day we heard of it, we have not ceased to pray for you and to ask that you may be filled with the knowledge of His will in all spiritual wisdom and understanding, so that you will walk in a manner worthy of the Lord, to please Him in all respects, bearing fruit in every good work and increasing in the knowledge of God; strengthened with all power, according to His glorious might, for the attaining of all steadfastness and patience; joyously giving thanks to the Father, who has qualified us to share in the inheritance of the saints in light. For He rescued us from the domain of darkness and transferred us to the kingdom of His beloved Son, in whom we have redemption, the forgiveness of our sins.

The Holy Spirit's Fifth Prayer for You

Again, God wants you to live with intentionality so that you can accomplish all His will. *2 Thessalonians 1:11-12* says:

> To this end also we pray for you always, that our God will count you worthy of your calling, and fulfill every desire for goodness and the work of faith with power, so that the name of our Lord Jesus will be glorified in you, and you in Him, according to the favour of our God.

The Holy Spirit's Sixth Prayer for You

When you appreciate and celebrate the good gifts that God has placed in you, your ministry becomes more effective. Listen to the prayer of the Spirit of God in *Philemon 1:6*: "And I pray that the fellowship of your faith may become effective through the knowledge of every good thing which is in you for Christ's sake."

The Holy Spirit's Seventh Prayer for You

The final prayer demonstrates God's desire for you to succeed in every area of your life. It also shows that a healthy heart is the key to a healthy and prosperous life. In *3 John 1:2*, the Holy Spirit prays with great tenderness for you: "Beloved, I pray that in all respects you may prosper and be in good health, just as your soul prospers."

What's on God's Heart?

Seven themes emerge in the seven prayers of the Holy Spirit. These are God's desires for your life and the things that He is constantly wanting for you. I will break them down as simply as possible so that you can get a fresh perspective of His heart for you.

Theme One - Knowing God

In four of these prayers, the Holy Spirit expresses His desire for you to grow in your knowledge of God. However well you know Jesus right now, He desires for you to come into a greater and deeper relationship with Him. He prays that the eyes of your heart will be opened to know and discern Him. He longs for you to be filled up with all the fullness of God, and for the presence of Christ to abide on the inside. What an awesome God we serve – that He desires an ever-increasing relationship with every one of us!

Theme Two - Your Calling

God will not give up on you. *Jeremiah 29:11* says: "'For I know the plans that I have for you', declares the Lord, 'plans for welfare and not for calamity to give you a future and a hope'." God has a phenomenal purpose for your life and is determined to see you fulfill your calling. In four of His prayers, the Holy Spirit intercedes for you to walk in His highest plans and purposes. Knowing the power of hope, He prays that your calling will inspire longing and desire. He prays that you will live a life that is worthy of your purpose, a life of righteousness and fruitfulness.

Theme Three - Supernatural Strength

Jesus understands the human condition. *Hebrews 4:15* says: "For we do not have a high priest who cannot sympathise with our weaknesses, but one who has been tempted in all things as we are, yet without sin." The Lord knows that you need supernatural strength to fulfil your purpose. In three of His prayers, the Holy Spirit intercedes for you to be strengthened deep down on the inside. He prays that the same power that raised Jesus from the dead, the very power of the Spirit of God, will infuse strength into your physical body. God does not just command us to be strong (*Joshua 1:9*), He prays for us to be supernaturally empowered.

Theme Four - Unshakable Love

It is not just that the Lord loves us. According to *1 John 4:8*, God is the very embodiment of love. It is, therefore, no surprise that He wants us to come into an ever-increasing knowledge of His love. He prays that the very roots, or foundations, of our Christian lives will be His love. The Holy Spirit prays that each one of us will come to know, by personal experience, the enormity of His love for us. Let's look at *Ephesians 3:17-19* in the *Amplified*:

...and may you, having been [deeply] rooted and [securely] grounded in love, be fully capable of comprehending with all the saints (God's people) the width and length and height and depth of His love [fully experiencing that amazing, endless love]; and [that you may come] to know [practically, through personal experience] the love of Christ which far surpasses [mere] knowledge [without experience].

It seems strange that the Lord would pray that we may know something that surpasses knowledge. The truth we discover through Paul the Apostle's knowledge of God is that the more we know of Him, the less we realise we know. *In Philippians 3:10*, Paul (who perhaps knew God better than anyone of his time), wrote: "I pray that I may know Him."

Theme Five - His Glory

God wants your life to reveal His glory. The Holy Spirit prays that the name of Jesus will be glorified through you. What a picture of the love and humility of the Trinity, the Spirit of God, praying that you and I will live lives that bring honor to the Son of God who paid such a high price. *2 Thessalonians 1:12* says He prays: "that the name of our Lord Jesus will be glorified in you." That God would glorify us with His own glory is almost impossible to believe. And yet He goes on to pray that "...you may be glorified in Him"!

Theme Six - True Health

It is not possible to freely acknowledge all the good things on the inside if you have low self-esteem. Two prayers reflect God's desire for you to have a healthy inner life. Whilst praying in *Philemon 1:6*, the Holy Spirit expresses His desire for you to be able to appreciate "every good thing which is in you in Christ Jesus." This flows from knowing your immense value as one created in the image and likeness of God (*Genesis 1:27*). The final prayer of the Spirit is revelatory. He prays for our prosperity and physical health, acknowledging that both flow from having a prosperous soul. Your soul is your mind, your will, and the seat of your emotions. It is your heart. *Proverbs 20:27* says: "The spirit of a man is the lamp of the Lord, searching all the inner depths of his heart." The Hebrew word translated 'depths' literally means rooms, chambers or caverns. Our souls are made up of many caverns or rooms. The Lord searches these hidden areas to uncover secret pain that may be blocking our prosperity or physical wellbeing. The Lord wants our heart to be healed of all life's hurts and disappointments because "…your heart determines the course of your life." (*Proverbs 4:23 NLT.*)

Theme Seven - Prosperity

The seventh prayer is both humbling and inspiring. The God of Heaven and Earth is praying that you will prosper in all areas of your life. The Greek word Euodoō features in *1 John 3:2*. It means to succeed.

God wants you to have successful relationships, a great ministry, a flourishing business, an excellent job. He prays for you to prosper and enjoy the abundant life that Jesus died to provide for you (*John 10:10*).

Praying With the Holy Spirit

These prayers should be on our lips every day. As you pray along with the Holy Spirit, you'll soak up His character, and His nature will become more real to you. The more you say these prayers, the more you will discover your value and identity as a child of God. The Holy Spirit spoke to me once, saying, "The biggest crisis in the body of Christ today is an identity crisis. You don't know who you are." When we set out on this identity quest, all the fake identities the world has pinned on us relating to ethnicity, skin colour, education, socioeconomic class, region etc., fall away.

2 Corinthians 5:17 says: "Therefore if anyone is in Christ, he is a new creature; the old things passed away; behold, new things have come." *The Old Testament* prophesied such a thing in *Psalms 102:18*: "This will be written for the generation to come, that a people yet to be created may praise the Lord." And again, *Ephesians 2:10* reads: "For we are His workmanship, created in Christ Jesus for good works, which God prepared beforehand so that we would walk in them." We know so little of our capabilities as a new creation. The Scripture continually challenges us to believe in our limitless abilities, making extraordinary statements like, "… we have the mind of Christ." (*1 Corinthians 2:16.*)

As we meditate on His word, we start to realise that we really are a new creation. Kingdom values, such as love, faith, and hope, carry more weight and importance than career, status, and the need to be accepted. As God showed me once, we need to become the 'one' in *1 John 3:16* (the first letter of John) which reads: "We know love by this, that He laid down His life for us; and we ought to lay down our lives for the brethren."

The more we soak up who we are as a new creation (it's a voyage of discovery and a great adventure), the more we become useful to our master, Jesus. It becomes easier to hear His voice as other voices of ambition, self-serving, self-aggrandisement, self-consciousness etc., fade into the distance. The more we allow the word of God to "dwell in us richly in all wisdom and understanding" (*Colossians 3:16*), the more it will change our thinking and help us to discern our master's voice over all other voices.

Imagine a soccer game: you're on the pitch as a player; you're surrounded by 60,000 fans all shouting at once, singing and waving their hands, or fists (depending which side you're on). But you are so focused and tuned into the game, you can hear a teammate's voice across the pitch calling for the ball. Imagine the level of focus, concentration and determination it takes to hear the right voices. It's the same for you and me. Scripture says that "There are many voices out there, and none without meaning." (*1 Corinthians 14:10*), so fine-tuning your spirit to His voice is a must. His priorities must become ours; His goals ours; His ways ours; His way of seeing things, ours. "Call wisdom your sister," the Bible says, "call understanding your close intimate friend." (*Proverbs 7:4.*)

I suggest you start saying these seven prayers daily. This will change your thinking, it will help you to see who you really are, and it will enable you to better understand the nature and heart of God.

Chapter 6

BAPTISED INTO
HIS VOICE

"The favour of the Lord Jesus Christ, the love of God, and the fellowship of the Holy Spirit be with you all, both now and forever, amen." So goes the blessing in *2 Corinthians 13:14*. If you have been in church longer than a few months, you will have heard this Scripture. But do we fellowship with Him? Do we invite Him to be a passenger in our car? Do we invite Him to watch TV with us? Do we give Him permission to speak to us, lead us and guide us in all our affairs? It is a great habit to get into.

Enjoying an evening at home, I watched a leisurely Sunday evening TV program set in a boatyard on the south coast of England. Wooden rowing boats were being hand fashioned using traditional skills, bending wood and hand sanding. These were things of beauty. The craftsman explained that such a vessel needed 24 layers of varnish. As he painted the first layer on, it disappeared totally into the wood, no sign of it at all. Only after coat number 12 did any varnish start to show. The Lord spoke to me in this: "So it is with My Word. Baptise yourself in My Word and let it sink down deep, layer upon layer."

Another time, I was watching a documentary on art restoration. A masterpiece had been found in a frame underneath another painting. A team were carefully removing the amateur picture hiding the work of art. The lady responsible for the restoration explained that she would spend an entire day working on a tiny area of the painting, about six square inches of canvas. The Lord spoke to me: "I am a master restorer of peoples' souls. However devastating the enemy's work on their lives, I can restore as if they were never wounded." *Amen to that*! I thought, not knowing the level of tragedy I would encounter in life and ministry. I'm so glad I got those revelations early on in my walk with the Lord. They came from inviting Him into my everyday life. Why not invite Him right now to lead every step you take.

True Fellowship

The Bible speaks about "the fellowship of our faith" in one of the prayers we studied in the previous chapter. This phrase found in *Philemon 1:6* speaks of the kind of intimate contact a mother enjoys while nursing her baby. That is the level of intimacy that the Lord desires to develop with His children; a closeness that changes you and envelopes you in His presence. Many times, we relate to our Heavenly

Father as though He is a reflection of our earthly father. If your dad was absent from your life or distant, you may struggle with doubt, especially self-doubt. If your father was harsh, cold or violent, then you may think your Heavenly Father is the same way. We must unlearn these things in the presence of the Lord and discover who our wonderful Holy Spirit is, the one fathering us now. Something phenomenal happens to us as we go through this process: we become more loving, more caring, more kind, more compassionate.

Let's break down that sixth prayer as an example (and don't worry if it's difficult to follow all chopped up as we'll piece it back together): "I pray" [this is the Holy Spirit praying for us] – "that the fellowship" – [literal Greek word *koinonia*, meaning intimacy (mother and nursing infant level intimacy] – "of your faith, may become full of power to achieve results, by the acknowledgment of every good thing that is in you by Christ Jesus." (*Philemon 1:6.*)

This one prayer prayed by the Holy Spirit and written by Paul, runs contrary to almost every teaching I had heard about how God sees us and how He wants us to see ourselves. Instead of seeing ourselves as unworthy worms or beggars, He wants us to acknowledge every good thing which is in us by Christ.

The result of seeing ourselves this way is that our faith becomes energised, *energeo*. In the Greek language (the original language of *The New Testament*), the word *energeo* is best thought of as the way we would charge our phone, plugged into a power source to revive and restore to full strength. We have been so robbed by religious teaching, it brings condemnation and guilt. No wonder so many of us lack spiritual power. Saying these seven prayers daily over yourself, your loved ones in Christ, your church, and your ministry will protect you. It is too easy to be deceived by wrong voices if you don't know His voice telling you who you are.

Chapter 7

FOLLOWING HIS LEADING

Much of this book is about learning to recognise and listen to the voice of God. There are other equally precious methods that the Lord uses to lead us by His Spirit. This chapter looks at some of the other ways that God guides us into His will.

Before going any further, I encourage you to pause briefly and read *1 John 2:20-27*. This passage reveals a dear gift given to believers which we call 'the inner witness'. *1 John 2:20 (KJV)* says: "But ye have an unction from the Holy One, and ye know all things." Other translations call that unction an anointing. In essence, the Bible teaches that we have an inner knowing that comes from the Holy Spirit. Here is the Scripture in its fullness: "But you have been anointed by [you hold a sacred appointment from, you have been given an unction from] the Holy One, and you all know [the truth] or you know all things." (*1 John 2:20 AMPC.*)

The Lord has deposited His Spirit deep in your heart as your guide. Just as a close friend might secretly prod you in public when they know something might help you, so the Holy Spirit wants you to tune in to His inner nudges. Later in this passage, we read: "But as for you, the anointing [the sacred appointment, the unction] which you received from Him abides [permanently] in you; [so], then you have no need that anyone should instruct you. But just as His anointing teaches you concerning everything and is true and is no falsehood, so you must abide in [live in, never depart from] Him [being rooted in Him, knit to Him], just as [His anointing] has taught you [to do]. (*1 John 2:27 AMPC.*)

Your Inner Tutor

Here, the Scripture is declaring that this inner 'anointing' can teach us and help us to know 'all things'. The greater our intimacy with the Holy Spirit, the more we will experience this inner unction. The word says that this anointing teaches us. So, we can understand that there is a reservoir of anointing *inside* us that reveals mysteries and guides us into all truth. It is an easy Scripture to go overboard on and say silly things like "I don't need anyone to teach me – I have the inner witness!" But that would mean that God is contradicting Himself by releasing one of the fivefold ministries, that of the teacher, into the earth "to equip the saints." (*Ephesians 4: 11-12.*) The inner witness does not replace the other ways God speaks; it is a wonderful addition.

The inner anointing is what recognises the truth. It is that little bell that rings in our hearts when the truth is shared. A good explanation of this is found in *2 Peter 1:12*: "Therefore, I will always be ready to remind you of these things, even though you already know them, and have been established in the truth which is present with you." That inner truth is the same residual anointing spoken of in *1 John 2:20*.

The Two-Edged Sword

Another way to be led by the Holy Spirit is by the Word of God, the Bible. "Contend with thy mother," says the Bible in *Hosea 2:2*. God gave me that Scripture one day. What a strange word to receive! I had been trying to contact my mum on the phone for several days beforehand and couldn't get through. Lo and behold when I saw that Scripture, I knew I'd get through, and I did, first time! Sometimes, it's the tiny things like this that not only demonstrate how the living Word of God works but demonstrate how intimately God loves and cares for us. It was a tiny, virtually irrelevant, matter, but 40 years later, I still remember that word from God like it was yesterday.

Get to know the Word of God inside out. It's amazing how much the Lord will speak to you and lead you through Scripture. Several years ago, my wife, Jo, began feeling that our house was too small for our growing family. We had been living there for 12 years.

I took it to God in prayer and opened my Bible to the following passage: "Now Solomon was building his own house thirteen years, and he finished all his house." (*1 Kings 7:1.*)

By the Scriptures and the inner witness, I knew that we should look for a bigger place in 2013, 13 years after we had moved to that house. We found a beautiful home with more accommodation. Not only that, but the buying process went as smoothly as silk. Why not start to ask God to lead you by His Word and the inner witness. It's a great way to live.

Prophecy

Prophecy is another way to follow the leading of the Holy Spirit. This subject could be a whole book on its own, but let me outline the basics:

1: Prophecy should be received from people who themselves have a good track record of following God.

2: Prophecy is for confirmation rather than information. If it's brand new to you and feels 'off', put it on the shelf and ask the Holy Spirit for confirmation. He doesn't look down on caution.

3: Prophecy should be in line with God's word. For instance, if someone prophesies that you will marry two wives at the same time, you know it is a goofy word because Jesus says marriage is between one man and one woman. That's an extreme example, but you get the point.

Getting to know the Word of God is of paramount importance if you're going to live a life directed by the Holy Spirit.

Chapter 8

ATTRIBUTES THAT ATTRACT GOD

"Serving will get you promoted into places you never could have reached otherwise." The Lord spoke these words to me clearly one day. Certain principles are so important to Christ that they attract the presence of God. Serving is one of them. It's amazing how underrated service is among God's people, and yet the Bible is full of people who were elevated into God's blessing by their service: Noah's building of the ark was practical service to mankind, and, as a result, God saved his family from the deluge; Rebecca's offer to water 10 of Abraham's camels (a camel can drink 20 gallons at a time) landed her a marriage to a billionaire and an eternal place in the patriarchy of God's chosen people; Joseph's way out of slavery and into recognition was through serving; David's arrival at his destiny appointment with Goliath was through serving. You can literally go through the Bible and notice the connection between serving and succeeding. The lesson? Find something to do in the body of Christ and do it like your life depended on it. I'm sure there are many jobs you could do in your church: you could help in the parking lot or nursery, join the welcome team, sign up to do some cleaning, or become an usher. Just make sure you are serving.

I've tried always to serve and be a blessing to people. A wonderful thing happened in a church I had been ministering at in Surrey, England. I had finished the service and was chatting with some people in the auditorium. As we spoke, I noticed out of the corner of my eye a young lady had pulled out a vacuum cleaner from a cupboard and started cleaning the floor. Suddenly, the heavens opened over her. I went over to her and started to prophesy great things to come. I declared the arrival of her papers to remain in the UK (I knew supernaturally she was 25 and was from Zambia). I saw the rejection and punishment she had gone through as a child and declared an end to those wounds. God hadn't spotlighted her in the service, but He recognised her in *her* service to Him. It reorganised my understanding of what it means to serve God, even in the most menial ways.

A Giving Heart

Determine to have a giving heart, always pouring out, always looking for ways to enhance people's lives. It is important in our quest to be led by The Holy Spirit that we attempt to imitate the heart of our Heavenly Father. It is much easier to hear the voice of The

Shepherd if we know what He's likely to say. Imitate God? you say. Yes! The Bible commands us to: "Therefore be imitators of God, as beloved children; and walk in love, just as Christ also loved you and gave Himself up for us, an offering and a sacrifice to God as a fragrant aroma." (*Ephesians 5: 1-2.*) The Greek word used for 'imitate' is the word phonetically spelt 'mimets', from where we get the word 'mimic'. The Holy Spirit is challenging us to mimic God. Did you ever find a pair of your parents' shoes and put them on as a child? Maybe your dad's hat or your mum's gloves? That's the intonation the Lord is giving us here: do things that are bigger than you in imitation of your Heavenly Father.

A God of Knowledge

Motives are very important to our Heavenly Father. Why we do what we do is as important as what we do for the Lord. "Our God is a God of knowledge and by Him, actions are weighed." (*1 Samuel 2:3.*) So spoke Hannah, the mother of Samuel, the mighty judge and prophet of Israel. He weighs what we do based upon why we are doing it. "The Word of God [a deliberate capital W] is living and active, sharper than any two-edged sword... and is a discerner of the thoughts and intents of the heart." (*Hebrews 4:12.*) As we read the Bible with an open heart, our intentions will be revealed so that we can purify our hearts. We need to be careful that we don't assume all our motives are pure. *Proverbs 21:2* says: "Every way of a man is right in his own eyes, but the Lord weighs the hearts." I encourage you to pause for a moment and ask the Holy Spirit to reveal to you the motives of *your* heart.

Integrity of Heart

Closely linked to motives, is integrity. *Psalms 41:12* says: "As for me, you uphold me in my integrity, and you set me in Your presence forever." What a promise! Transparency of heart and motive can set you like a seal on the heart of our God forever! This verse also suggests that integrity attracts the presence of the Lord. This is important to know when you walk through tough times. The Bible calls such seasons 'the hour of darkness' or 'the evil day'. In such times, it is extremely hard to hear God, so you need to be led by your principles and by your training. I imagine it must feel similar for a pilot flying into a storm: they can't see anything outside but know to depend on the internal gauges and controls to navigate through successfully. It is a good idea to set your controls beforehand, as the Bible says: "Therefore, let everyone who is godly pray to You in a time when You may be found; surely in a flood of great waters they will not reach him." (*Psalm 32:6.*) Walking in integrity provides a pathway: the straight and narrow way that leads to life. When you protect your integrity and refuse to compromise, the Lord will stay close to you and lead you in to all His will.

Chapter 9

THE 'F' WORD

There's something at work on the inside of us that goes against our desire to be right with God: our flesh. It attempts to reign in our minds (carnality), in our bodies (lust), and in our souls (soulishness). It fights the will of God in multiple ways. If it can't stop you by holding you back, it will try, by various impulses, to push you too far. It will throw feelings into the plan of God like a 'spanner in the works'; it will make you react to spiritual things in emotional ways, especially relationships; it will try to get you addicted to food, alcohol, medication, drugs, pornography, gossip (which is soulful pornography), a life of comfort and ease – the list is endless.

Your Soul

Let's look at the original purpose of your soul. Your soul is an interface between your spirit and the natural realm. Your soul is made up of your mind, your will and your emotions. Your mind is where your thoughts and imaginations function. *Proverbs 21:7* says: "…as a man thinks in his heart, so is he" So, our thinking has spiritually-generative power. Our deep-seated thoughts can affect the way we behave. Our mind is the place where reason (in most people anyway!) resides. *Luke 1:46* states a central purpose of the human soul: "My soul magnifies the Lord, and my spirit has rejoiced in God my Saviour." The original purpose of your soul is to magnify God, thereby amplifying our awareness of Him in the natural realm. Just like a prism divides the full visible spectrum of light, so your soul has been created to amplify the beauty, majesty, creativity, tenderness, greatness, and kindness of our Heavenly Father into the natural realm.

Emotional damage can distort our inner image of God, it can damage our view of ourselves, and it affects our opinion of the world around us. It is vital that we learn how to receive healing for our souls. If the devil has successfully crippled your emotions, broken your will, or contaminated your mind, he can exercise jurisdiction in these areas. It is only when our damaged souls are healed that his authority is annulled. My wife has dedicated her life to working in this realm of healing the soul and I believe that her ministry is one of the foremost in the world on this issue. Her books, courses and materials are available at wholeheartministries.net.

In one of the seven prayers, The Holy Spirit prays that you "… may prosper and be in health, even as your soul prospers." (*3 John 1:2.*) Our wellbeing and well-doing are directly connected to the health of our souls (our minds, wills and emotions). Soulishness is when we become fixated on physical or emotional aspects of life, as opposed to spiritual matters. Our fleshly nature attaches itself to the unredeemed, uncleansed parts of our souls and we become soulish. For example, if you fell in love with everyone who showed you even the slightest bit of attention before you got saved, then it's quite possible you have carried that trait over into your born-again experience. Your spirit has been reborn, but your soul can carry you off into the arms of the wrong person. You could be relating emotionally to people that God has placed in your life as spiritual brothers and sisters. If you were impulsive before you got saved, unless you allow God to work on your soul, you'll still be impulsive until you "cease striving and know that I Am God." (*Psalm 46:10.*)

Enemies of the Soul

Carnality is a destiny killer and curtailer. It often blocks our ears to the voice of the Spirit and blinds our eyes to His leading. From the Latin word meaning 'of the flesh' or 'fleshly', carnality has 1001 manifestations: gossip, overeating, drunkenness, lewdness – the list goes on. All of these can individually, or collectively, become destiny destroyers. Fasting is a great carnality crusher. People who talk too much should fast more! If your body mass index is over the recommended size for your frame, fasting will help you to pull your physical body into subjection to the will of God.

The Holy Spirit, through Paul the Apostle, describes the kind of relationship we (the real us, the spirit 'us' that inhabits our physical bodies) should have with our physical body. *1 Corinthians 9:27* states: "I discipline my body and make it my slave, so that, after I have preached to others, I myself will not be disqualified." Paul made his physical body a slave to the purposes of God and that's what we need to do, too. Part of the problem in the body of Christ is that there are far too many runaway slaves! If you want to be successfully led by the Holy Spirit, you must bring your body into line. You need to learn to ignore its desire for comfort, for constant feeding, and for things that are bad for you. You need to stop letting your body have everything it wants and train it as though you were breaking in a horse.

Let's look at how the Holy Spirit describes this war and enmity. *Romans 8: 5-8* says: "For those who are carnal (according to the flesh) set their minds on the things of the flesh, but those who are according to the Spirit, the things of the Spirit. For the mind set on the flesh is death, but the mind set on the Spirit is life and peace, because the mind set on the flesh is hostile toward God; for it does not subject itself to the law of God, for it is not even able to do so, and those who are in the flesh cannot please God."

Entertainment, comfort and the 'must-have-three-meals-a-day' lifestyle can dominate the born-again believer and cause them to miss God. We need to be led by the Spirit of God (*Romans 8:14*) not by our cravings and impulses. What we tolerate will dominate.

And now to lust. We mostly associate lust with sexual sin, and this is largely justified by how driven we (particularly men) can be by such urges. However, to put lust in such a box is to miss its essence. In its most basic form, lust is pressure, coming from our flesh or soulish nature, to do the wrong things. Lust enters through what we think, what we see, what we feel, or what we hear. The devil analyses our weakness, often through generational lines, and attempts to pollute or control us through lust. The Holy Spirit, through Paul the Apostle, puts it this way: "I was once alive apart from the Law; but when the commandment came, sin became alive and I died." (*Romans 7:9.*)

Temptation is the test of our ability to resist that pressure. There is always an escape route when temptation comes, so it's wise to look for off-ramps if you find yourself on temptation's highway. *1 Corinthians 10:13 (NIV)* is very reassuring: "No temptation has overtaken you except what is common to mankind. And God is faithful; he will not let you be tempted beyond what you can bear. But when you are tempted, he will also provide a way out so that you can endure it."

There is a lot of wrong teaching concerning temptation. It is, therefore, a good exercise to note down all the verses on this subject and make sure you know what your Heavenly Father is talking about. I will use this topic to show you the importance of understanding Scripture within the light of Scripture. For the Bible to be wholly true concerning temptation in the New Covenant, we need to see the Lord's Prayer as a declaration rather than a supplication prayer. Let me explain.

Translating Scripture in the Light of Scripture

Let's look at it now.

> Our Father who art in Heaven, hallowed be your name. Your Kingdom come, Your will be done on Earth as it is in Heaven. [You] give us this day, our daily bread, and [you] forgive us our trespasses as we forgive those who trespass against us. (You) lead us not into temptation but [you] deliver[ed] us from evil. For thine is the Kingdom and the power and the glory forever and ever. Amen. (*Luke 11:1-4.*)

By adding the word 'you', we have turned the Lord's Prayer into a declaration that reflects New Covenant teaching. Let me explain something important: although the *New Testament* started with the gospel of Matthew, the New Covenant began after the death, burial and resurrection of Jesus Christ.

So, back to the Lord's Prayer. Why would we ask God not to do something He already promises He would not do? *James 1:13* says: "Let no one say when he is tempted, 'I am being tempted by God'; for God cannot be tempted by evil, and He Himself does not tempt anyone."

Let's now look at *Colossians 1:13*: "For He has delivered us from the domain of darkness and translated us into the kingdom of the son of His love." So why pray "deliver us from evil?" Rightly dividing The Word of Truth (as the Holy Spirit calls the Scriptures) is very necessary when listening out for the voice of the Holy Spirit. There are many deceptive voices out there and unless your knowledge of the Word is doctrinally sound, you could end up sacrificing your child on a mountain somewhere, convinced that it was the voice of the Lord who instructed you.

Rightly Dividing the Word of Truth

Failing to rightly divide the Word of Truth is the source of many deceptions. We must factor in the dispensation we live under—the dispensation of favour—at all times. For those under the dispensation of the law, for instance, eating pig meat was forbidden, along with all kinds of animals. Under the dispensation of favour, God spoke to Peter, saying "kill and eat," (*Acts 10:13*) so we are able to enjoy that bacon and egg McMuffin! Polygamy was common under the dispensation of the law. Jesus Christ restored the dignity of woman lost by Adam's fall. He taught us that Christian marriage should be between one man and one woman and (with very few off-ramps, known as divorce) last for life. (For the sake of clarity, a man is a biological male, and a woman is a biological female.)

Chapter 10

SET APART FOR THE MASTER'S USE

If there is one instruction I would give to anyone who wants to get to know God, it would be this: become a worshipper. Spend quality time in God's presence, one on one, and worship Him. You may not be able to sing a note or play an instrument, but one thing I have observed in my four (so far) decades in Christ is that worshippers make it through. Parts of your Christian journey are going to be rough—betrayals, disappointments, accusations, or mistakes may be round the corner—but if you're a worshipper, God will pull you through as you stay close to Him.

Worship brings Heaven's atmosphere to Earth, it attracts the presence of God, and it sensitises the human spirit to Him. If you are going to hear, and be led by, the Holy Spirit, make worship your lifestyle. The world has its own sound; it is in our stores, shopping centres, TV adverts, and food courts. You need a different sound. As you worship, you will create a heavenly atmosphere around you, you will clear the spiritual airwaves, making way for His presence, His voice, His blessing. You will be separating yourself unto the Lord.

Guard Your Heart

Every week, the pastor of one of the biggest churches in America, Joel Osteen, asks the Holy Spirit to search his heart. Joyce Meyer shared that for every three steps forward, she stops for a heart check. We must be sober, and watchful, always. *Proverbs 4:23* says: "Diligently guard your heart above all things, for from it flow the forces of life." The devil has been at this game a long time. If Satan can't hold you back, he'll try to push you too far; if he can't keep you impoverished, he'll try to corrupt you with wealth; if he can't persecute you with hatred, he'll try to make you a cult figure. All of these can pollute our hearts.

Paul and Barnabas endured crazy reactions from the crowds at Lystra. *Acts 14:8-13* tell the story:

> At Lystra a man was sitting who had no strength in his feet, lame from his mother's womb, who had never walked. This man was listening to Paul as he spoke, who, when he had fixed his gaze on him and had seen that he had faith to be made well, said with a loud voice, 'Stand

upright on your feet'. And he leaped up and began to walk.

When the crowds saw what Paul had done, they raised their voice, saying in the Lycaonian language, 'The gods have become like men and have come down to us'. And they began calling Barnabas, Zeus, and Paul, Hermes, because he was the chief speaker. The priest of Zeus, whose temple was just outside the city, brought oxen and garlands to the gates, and wanted to offer sacrifice with the crowds.

Firstly, they had to guard their hearts from the temptation to lap up the people's praises.

Just a few hours later, public opinion changed. We will pick the story back up at verse 19: "But Jews came from Antioch and Iconium, and having won over the crowds, they stoned Paul and dragged him out of the city, supposing him to be dead." In one day, they went from adulation to murderous hatred. Both are forms of persecution, both can cause our motives to be tested.

As we guard our hearts and check that our motives are pure, we can rest assured that the Lord will watch our ways. *Jude 24* says: "Now to Him who is able to keep you from stumbling and present you blameless unto God... to Him be the glory majesty dominion and authority before all time and forever more." We must lean heavily on His ability, His direction and His protection. By our surrender, we access these great gifts from God.

Not an Optional Extra!

Fasting is a great separator. Some of us have been taught from an early age that every desire of our eyes or appetite is good and should be answered. As a result, our flesh nature gains ascendancy through our appetites. This is wrong and our flesh nature needs imprisonment and enslavement. I tell my physical body what and when to eat, just like I filter what I allow my mind to think. Medical science has told us for several generations that we eat too much and too often. As disciples of Christ, if we are medically able to do so, I believe we should fast at least one day a week and watch what we eat when we do eat. Fat, sugar and salt are risky substances and should be consumed with care.

Let's look again at *1 Corinthians 9:27*: "I discipline my body and make it my slave, so that, after I have preached to others, I myself will not be disqualified." The original Greek word 'disqualified' denotes 'being rejected as a counterfeit'. I don't know about you, but I don't want to reach the finish line in this life and face disqualification because I allowed my flesh to dominate. I refuse to permit my physical nature to become a runaway slave.

If you are serious about living your life for God, fasting is a must. When He was teaching on the subject, Jesus did not say, *if* you fast; He said, *when* you fast. Fasting enables you to train your flesh and bring it into slavery. Make no mistake, your flesh nature is an enemy of the God nature taking root in you. Fasting helps you subdue your flesh. It's a necessity for every believer.

It's a Journey

I remember the first day I fasted. I thought I was going to die. And it was only 9.30am! Previously, I could go until 3pm and not even think about food, but now? It took just two hours for me to be ravenous. My flesh was rebelling, and it was time to bring it under subjection. Let me repeat the verse again: "...but I discipline my body and *make it my slave*, so that, after I have preached to others, I myself will not be disqualified." I had a runaway slave and so started a war with my flesh nature. From now on I would tell it when it was allowed to eat, when it was allowed to sleep, when it could be entertained.

I ended up going overboard, with such a harsh disciplinary lifestyle that God had to divinely intervene with this Scripture: "...for no one ever hated his own flesh but nourishes and cherishes it." (*Ephesians 5:29.*) I was fasting three days a week and living a seriously rigorous lifestyle. In His mercy, God slowed me down. I learned something important from that season in my life: if the devil can't hold you back, he'll try to push you too far. If he can't push you into a ditch one way, he'll try the other. If he can't stop you on the road, he'll try to bend the road. We shouldn't be ignorant of his devices.

Ask the Holy Spirit to introduce you to a prayer and fasting regime that will help you to achieve your destiny. He knows you; He formed your inward parts. For me, this unfolded over time and set me on a trajectory that has brought about countless testimonies to the glory of His name. My prayer is that this will be the same for you in Jesus's name.

Guided Giving

Your giving should be led by the Holy Spirit too. Without His guidance, you can end up giving too little, too much, or in the wrong situations. Just because there's a need, doesn't mean you're the one who should meet it; just because there isn't a need, doesn't mean that you shouldn't be giving. Some of my biggest financial seeds have been into ministries that are carrying a surplus. Necessity and compulsion are bad reasons to give according to the Scriptures. *2 Corinthians 9:6-7* is clear: "Now this I say, he who sows sparingly will also reap sparingly, and he who sows bountifully will also reap bountifully. Each one must do just as he has purposed in his heart, not grudgingly or under compulsion, for God loves a cheerful giver."

Financial Farming

The Lord compares the giving of our finances to 'sowing', the way that a farmer would plant seed, deliberately and purposefully, with the expectation of a harvest. Farmers always sow what they want to reap. Jesus describes the 'sowing' of His own life as a seed, with the expectation of reaping a harvest of souls. In *John 4:24-25*, Jesus said: "Truly, truly, I say to you, unless a grain of wheat falls into the earth and dies, it remains alone; but if it dies, it bears much fruit. He who loves his life loses it, and he who hates his life in this world will keep it to life eternal."

Seedtime and harvest-thinking is a really good way to approach life and giving in general. The Holy Spirit, through Paul, says this to us in *Galatians 6:7-8*:

> Do not be deceived, God is not mocked; for whatever a man sows, this he will also reap. For the one who sows to his own flesh will from the flesh reap corruption, but the one who sows to the Spirit will from the Spirit reap eternal life.

I see my giving as financial farming; I see the giving of my life to Christ daily as sowing my life as a seed; I see my actions as determining future outcomes. What a great way to live!

Cleaning Out

As we seek to draw near to God, we must rid ourselves of deception and decontaminate our lives of any past contact with the spirit realm. The devil has always tried to make his stuff appealing to young people – tarot cards, Ouija boards, palm reading, astrology, drug culture etc., are all demonic counterfeits of the realm of the Holy Spirit. Satan tries to repackage things like divination to become young and trendy to a gullible group. If you have ever been involved in such things, renounce them and cut yourself off from them completely. Any mementos, books, charms, articles or utensils once used in spiritist activities need to be destroyed. Prayerfully discard any gifts received from witches.

Before he got saved, one of my mentors was given two magic stones by a guy he met in a café. He was told: "These stones will bring you great wealth! Keep them on you always and don't lose them or give them away until you know when and who to." He did it for a laugh at first. However, soon after he received these stones, he got a business idea, opened eight big stores in two years, paid off a huge mortgage, and bought himself a new Rolls Royce. He never equated his success to the weird occurrence with the stones.

When this man gave his live to Jesus, he joined a charismatic renewal prayer group in his town. On his first visit, the pastor received a word of knowledge that there was something hindering the visitation

God into someone's life. He stated that they needed to dispose of something in their possession by fire. He went on to describe accurately how the 'gift' was given. My mentor realised it was him and asked for prayer. He gave the stones to the pastor for destruction by fire which happened that night. Three months later, my mentor lost his business and was declared bankrupt. A few years ago, I was listening to the radio while on vacation in Miami, Florida, and heard a virtually identical story.

Objects That Have Been Dedicated to Idols

Some jewellery dedicated to gods, ancient Egyptian signs and symbols, astrology articles, and other memorabilia can be points of contact for demonic entities to influence people. A pastor once told me the story of a missionary couple in their church who, upon returning from Africa, bought a tribal mask from a roadside vendor. They hung it in their dining room over a dresser near their fruit bowl. Upon awaking the following day, all the fruit was gone! They got a bit freaked out so put the mask in their bag ready for the charity store. After they dropped off the mask to the charity shop, the store burned down.

Upon visiting a stop-off area in Kenya, I was chatting with a store owner about the masks he was selling. "Are you a Christian?" he asked before continuing. "These masks aren't for Christians. Witches place the masks over a child, kill the child, and use the power of the blood for their rituals. They then sell the masks to businesspeople for power." These things are real! We even see some individuals in the music industry using their stages and arenas to resemble Hell's gates and to create satanic altars. The Bible says to "avoid every semblance of evil." Best to stay safe and, if in doubt, throw it out.

Covenants and Contamination

If you participated in any blood rituals or covenants, you'll need to renounce them by the superior blood of Jesus Christ and take communion for your separation from these things. Drug culture is another thing to renounce. Weed, excessive alcohol and hard drugs can put you over into the realm of the spirit in a dangerous and damaging way. That's why the devil promotes it. The devil will always promote things that end up killing, robbing or destroying lives. Jesus is the Good Shepherd. If you follow His leading, He will lead you into great things.

If you've ever been to séance meetings, fortune-tellers, witches, diviners, better to be safe than sorry – cut yourself off from them with prayer and move on. For this reason, I don't engage in homeopathic remedies, acupuncture, even tattoos. I may be 'old school', but I love the Holy Spirit too much to be engaged in those things. If there's even a whiff in Scripture that these things may be 'off', I'm not risking it.

A few years ago, I was in Mozambique ministering at a big crusade. After the meetings were finished, a few dignitaries held a thank you dinner for us. The police chief's wife told us that in rural areas it wasn't uncommon to hear stories of mothers bringing one of their children to a witch to become a human sacrifice for wealth, power and prosperity. I was horrified. Then the Lord spoke to me: "The same happens in 'civilised' places," He said. "A woman in a high paid job who doesn't want to break her career path and sees having a baby as an interruption, will go and seek an abortion. Both will face the same standard of judgement before Me. Blood is blood."

If you have ever played a part in abortion, even complicity by encouraging someone else, even giving them a lift to the clinic, make sure you confess and renounce your sin to the Lord. Blood is a unique substance in the realm of the spirit and represents life to God. Do not be complicit with the deeds of darkness. *Revelation 9:20-21* lists some of the atrocities that can attract the wrath of God: "The rest of mankind, who were not killed by these plagues, did not repent of the works of their hands, so as not to worship demons, and the idols of gold and of silver and of brass and of stone and of wood, which can neither see nor hear nor walk, and they did not repent of their murders nor of their sorceries nor of their immorality nor of their thefts." Make sure your life is clean and clear of all connection with these things.

Connected to Christ

Water baptism can separate us from past sin and raise us up in newness of life. Prayer meetings (if they're led by spiritual people) will help draw you into a closer relationship with the Lord. Worship, which is abundantly available on music streaming services, will bring you into the presence of God. Why not ask the Holy Spirit to bring you into a time of separation to Him. Ask Him to show you anything that may be a hindrance to you hearing His voice. Times of sanctification usher you into a wonderful season.

We spend years at school and college trying to learn things that will help us get to the next level of life, but how many of us have actually devoted serious time to reach new heights in our relationship with Jesus Christ? The Lord wants us to reach the point where we know the voice, the presence and the absence of our Heavenly Father. I've been through several seasons like this, all of them being preludes to a greater knowledge of God. There's nothing like it!

Chapter 11

HIS PRESENCE

"I saw the Lord always in my presence; for He is at my right hand, so that I will not be shaken." (*Acts 2:25.*)

Early on in my walk with God, a deep desire to know the Holy Spirit grew in my heart. *Jeremiah 29:13* says: "And you will seek me and find me, when you search for me with all your heart." I knew I had to be all in, so I set time aside to fast, and devoted an hour each day after work to being alone with the Lord. That's the context to the encounter I described at the start of this book. (There is always a backstory to every visitation of God's glory.) So, there I was, aged 20, sitting alone on my bed with my hands resting in my lap facing up. Even my body language was telling the Lord that I was longing and waiting to receive something.

I sat in silence with my eyes closed, quietening even my thoughts as best I could. *Psalm 62:1* was guiding me: "Truly my soul silently waits for God; from Him comes my salvation." On the fourth day, as I sat with my eyes closed, gently worshipping the Lord, I saw what looked like the light from a lantern in the distance coming towards me. As I called upon His name, the light got brighter and closer until I was completely enveloped in His glorious presence.

"You wanted to experience my presence," the Lord said to me sometime later. "But first you had to know my absence." I knew right then that God was training me to be sensitive to His spirit; He was training me for ministry. I became more and more alert to His presence. I began to understand the different 'presences'of God: whether He was there to judge, to heal, to exhort, to bring blessing, to do miracles, or to release giftings and callings.

Get to know the Holy Spirit for yourself. To help you on your journey, I recommend two books by Benny Hinn: *Good Morning Holy Spirit* and *The Anointing*. He was a spiritual mentor to me for many years, then, by divine providence, I ended up becoming his UK ministry director, travelling with him and fellowshipping with him many times. It was a tremendous privilege.

Hunger For More

Prayer meetings in the early days of my salvation provided great spiritual training. Twice a year, we would jump on a coach from Galway in the west of Ireland to the capital city of Dublin. We would stay at our mentor's house for a weekend of prayer and fellowship. It was always exciting to meet brothers and sisters in the Lord and gather for times of prayer. I developed a hunger for the gifts of the Holy Spirit and watched closely as our leader, Paul Kelly, would lay hands on people, prophesy and 'see things'.

A story I mentioned earlier warrants a revisit. I wanted to move in the gifts too and reasoned to myself why not? If it really is God doing these things, then I can see them too. I can prophesy, too. *1 Corinthians 14:1* says: "Earnestly desire the spiritual gifts, especially that you may prophesy." So, I pressed in hard to that dimension. Then, lo and behold, at one meeting, while we were standing in a circle, eyes closed, Paul was going round ministering as the Holy Spirit was leading him. I opened my eyes while praying and saw a pathway above a woman's head, winding along and leading to great blessing.

"I see a pathway opening up before you," said Paul as he got to her, "a winding path, and it's leading to great blessing." *Bingo!* I exclaimed in my heart. I knew I had broken through into that realm. Accessing the spiritual gifts is like that, like tunnelling and then breaking through. The spiritual gifts are essential in the body of Christ today. We are so good at presentation, so slick in delivery, so polished in front of cameras. But the gifts of the Holy Spirit are what is needed to bring His glory to this generation. Anyone can talk.

Your Priorities

If you still want to hear and follow the leading of the Holy Spirit, you are going to have to put this activity first. There are a few words in the Bible which, because of the way they've been translated, have become a hindrance rather than a connector for our faith. Words like grace, baptise, and gospel are used almost exclusively in a Christian context. As a result, they don't mean much in the real world. Words are important. They are containers that carry faith and hope to the human heart; they are transmission mechanisms that bring Heaven to Earth and the realm of the spirit to the natural world.

Re-translating these words into everyday language is vital so that they can transmit what the Master is communicating to our spirits. One such is the word 'seek'. If we don't know what it means to seek, how can we do it? To seek, in its 21st-century form means 'to prioritise'. Here's a little challenge: reread every Scripture you know about 'seeking' and put the word 'prioritise' in its place. Then see what changes in your understanding about the attitude God wants us to have towards Him.

"Prioritise first the Kingdom of God and its righteousness and all these things (everything the world prioritises, the nice stuff) shall be added to you," says *Matthew 6:33*. How much richer would God's people be if they got their priorities right? Doing such a thing is not easy—it can take years to grow in the things of God—but with the constant pressure of faith, the continual declarations of faith, and the commitment to prioritise God's voice in your life, it will come to pass.

Don't Give up, Ever

PUSH is an anagram for Pray Until Something Happens. It will take relentless prayer, faith and a whole lot of perseverance to fine-tune your ear into God's voice. Our priorities can be regularly tested, especially when there is a conflict of urgency: your tithe needs to go out, but your car tyre needs replacing. Or there's a party invite but it's a church prayer meeting night. Or it's time to leave home for church but it's raining. Young girls run the risk of being raped every time they go to church in Pakistan but still their churches are full. How are your priorities? It takes commitment to become accustomed to the voice of the Lord.

In this age of entitlement, I make sure that anyone who works for the ministry has a full job description. It must encompass everything that will cover personal development and every eventuality that may arise. The job description consists of two words: Whatever's Necessary. It's an issue of priorities.

Prayers That Move Heaven

In the realm of prayer, your heart is the launchpad of your prayers. It is therefore vital that the priorities of your heart are as aligned as possible with God's priorities. Prayer is not twisting God's arm; it is aligning our will to His. The length of time you pray, passion, and persistence are three vital ingredients to a successful prayer life. "I thank my God I pray in tongues more than you all," says Paul in *1 Corinthians 14:18*, making it clear that the length of time you spend praying in other tongues matters. Then, in *James 5:16*, we learn about the value of passion: "The fervent effectual prayer of a righteous man makes tremendous power available, dynamic in its working." In *Luke 18:1-7*, Jesus taught about the importance of persistence in prayer and explained that our petitions must be filled with faith. Jesus would often pray all night.

Our monthly all-night meetings at Harvest Church have been the venue for many a conquest. God has directed us to overthrow terrorist armies, declare war, declare peace, expose terror plots, quench riots, release blessings, uplift politicians, and help change the course of history. Fervent effectual prayer is potent when it is led by the Spirit of God.

Tuning in

Unveiling the future is part of the ministry of the Holy Spirit through us, according to *John 16:13* and *Ephesians 3:10*. "He will take from what is mine," declares Jesus, "and He will show you things to come." You can't get clearer than that. God wants to tell you what will happen. We may know in part, see in part, and prophesy in part, but those 'parts' will often be enough for us to know what's around the corner. We just need to be sensitive enough and spiritual enough to tune into the voice of God. Old transistor radios had one button for tuning into the frequency desired and another 'fine-tuning' button. That second button enabled the listeners to home in on an exact station with near perfect clarity. It is just like that in the spiritual realm.

"There are many voices, and none without meaning," says the Holy Spirit through Paul in *1 Corinthians 14:10*, or we would say 'there are many radio stations out there, so tune into the right one'. The more you devour the word of God, surround yourself with the atmosphere of worship, lock out the world and all its distractions (*1 John 2:16*), work on the contents of your heart (*Mark 4: 1-20, Matthew 13: 1-23, Luke 8: 4-15*) and get your priorities right (*Matthew 6: 33*), you'll find tuning into God becomes a part of your spirit nature. Most advanced civilisations on this planet now have mobile phones, enabling instant and easy contact. Our communication with God must be an equally integral part of our lives.

Find Your Niche

Developing a healthy prayer life that suits you is essential. People pray in different ways. Because of the call of God on our lives, my wife and I rarely spend extended times together in prayer. Please don't misunderstand me – a family that prays together, stays together. Praying together should be the rule, but we were an exception. Because of the different ministries God has given us, I would spend my prayer time fellowshipping with the Holy Spirit and meditating on His word. She would be all tears and snot!

Allow the Holy Spirit to mould your prayer life. You may be a praiser – the great Apostle of Miracles, Smith Wigglesworth, used to dance before the Lord for 15 minutes a day every morning. "I never usually pray for more than five minutes," answered Wigglesworth when asked how often he prayed, "but I never usually go five minutes without praying." Dedicating your times of prayer to the Lord may seem like a no-brainer, but it is surprising how many people have never done it. If that's you, why don't you pause right now and give God your prayer life.

Bible study is similar. I've ministered in churches where the leader has said that unless the congregation is reading five chapters a day, he doubts they're saved. But just as we will each have a unique prayer life, we will probably all study the word of God slightly differently. I don't usually manage more than one paragraph! Because of the richness that each verse carries, I digest each phrase as though I'm studying law. I desire to see the entirety of each word come to pass in my experience.

Ask the Holy Spirit to lead and guide you into the word of God. See how it comes alive. Pray the *Ephesians 1* prayer over your life and watch the spirit of wisdom and revelation bring the Scriptures to life.

It's transformational. The more you know and understand the Word, the easier you will find discerning the voice of God.

As I bring this book to a close, I want to encourage you that a glorious journey lies ahead of you if you pursue more of the Holy Spirit in your life. His presence makes the difference. He lights up even painful walks through dark valleys. He is the way, the truth and He is life itself.

I would love to lead you in prayer:

Heavenly Father

I want to hear Your voice. I want to follow the leading of Your Holy Spirit in a real and living way. Help me to know Your word and teach me how to become a true servant of yours. I declare that as one of Your sheep, I will hear Your voice, I will know Your voice, I will follow Your voice, and the voice of another, I simply will not follow. Help me to hear Your voice for the benefit of others.

Speak to me in Truth by the Spirit of Truth, Your blessed Holy Spirit. I desire to become more like Jesus by following your leading. I desire to be used by Your Spirit to be a blessing to others. By hearing Your voice, I know I will become a better, more loving Christian and an example to others. May that be my testimony.

In Jesus's mighty name, I pray.

Amen.

AN INVITATION

If you have picked up this book and you have not yet made a commitment to follow Jesus Christ, please say this prayer:

Dear Lord

I know that you love me and have a wonderful plan for my life. I ask you to come into my heart today and be my saviour and Lord. Forgive me for all my sins, I pray. Thank you that because you died on the cross for me, I am forgiven of every wrong I have ever committed when I repent. I give my life to you entirely and ask you to lead me in your ways from now on.

In Jesus's name.

Amen.

If you have said this prayer for the first time, it will be important to tell a Christian friend what you prayed and to find a good church. Just as a newborn baby needs nourishment and care, so you (and all Christians) need the support of other believers as you start your new life as a follower of Jesus Christ.

You can watch free Bible messages that will help to build your faith by subscribing to Harvest Church London's YouTube channel. You can follow Paul on Instagram @paulnaughton_

God bless you!

ABOUT THE AUTHOR

Paul Naughton followed the call of God into full-time ministry after a successful career in banking. He has preached in major crusades, at conferences, and in churches in 27 nations across four continents. Paul has great authority in the Word and moves under a strong prophetic anointing, bringing the supernatural power of God with signs following. He has been featured on television and radio networks across Europe, Africa, and the Americas. He is founder and senior pastor of Harvest Church in London, England, which he leads, together with his wife, Jo. Paul is passionate about raising mighty prayer warriors in the UK.

Paul and Jo have two wonderful children, Benjy and Abby.

You can connect with Paul via www.harvestchurch.org.uk YouTube (Harvest Church London) or Instagram (@paulnaughton_)

OTHER BOOKS BY THE AUTHOR:

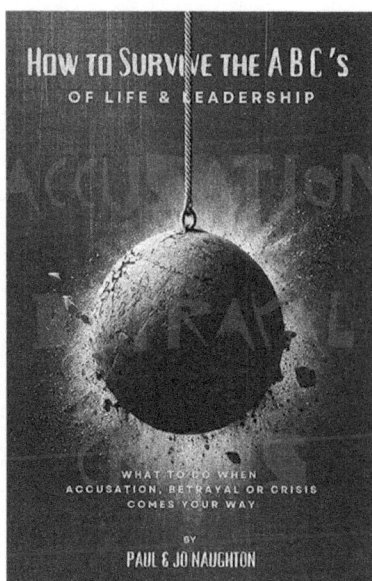

HOW TO RISE FROM THE ASHES OF

TRAGEDY

BY PAUL & JO NAUGHTON

HOW TO SURVIVE THE A B C's
OF LIFE & LEADERSHIP

WHAT TO DO WHEN
ACCUSATION, BETRAYAL OR CRISIS
COMES YOUR WAY

BY
PAUL & JO NAUGHTON